The 40s

Compiled by Murray Brown

Copyright © Jane's Publishing Company Limited 1984

First published in the United Kingdom in 1984 by
Jane's Publishing Company Limited
238 City Road, London EC1V 2PU

ISBN 0 7106 0305 3

Typeset by D. P. Media Ltd, Hitchin, Hertfordshire

Printed by Toppan Printing Co (S) Pte Ltd
38 Liu Fang Road, Jurong, Singapore 2262

JANE'S

Cover illustrations

Front: No 40198 stands at Newcastle Central after arrival with the
Manchester–Newcastle newspaper train on 9 May 1981. (*Fred Kerr*)

Rear: After restoration but before application of yellow warning
panels, No 40122 poses at Toton on 22 July 1983. (*Murray Brown*)
Yashica 124G   Ektachrome 64   1/250, f4

Right: Despite lacking an official allocation of 40s for some years,
Crewe has remained a haven for the class. Present at Crewe Diesel
Depot on 17 February 1978 was No 40177. Delivered new to Camden
in February 1962, this machine was one of a small batch
(Nos 40170–40177) which were the first locomotives fitted with dual
braking (of a design now considered non-standard) for working the
early Freightliner trains. (*Barry J Nicolle*)
Olympus OM1   Agfa CT18   1/125, f5.6

Introduction

In March 1958, some gangers were working at Conisborough, between Sheffield and Doncaster. They heard a horn but took no notice and suddenly had to jump for their lives, leaving still *in situ* a jack which duly ripped the AWS receiver from a 133-ton gleaming green locomotive and which caused it to stop with loss of power in Conisborough tunnel. 'Didn't you hear the horn?' the gangers were asked. They replied, 'We thought it was a barge on the canal'. D200 had arrived to begin the reign of one of the most successful diesel classes on BR.

The English Electric Company Type 4, later to be known as the Class 40, has certainly endured the passage of time extremely well and its impressive looks have not dated. D200 and its first nine sisters each cost £100,000 and the class of 200 units undoubtedly has proved to be one of BR's best bargains from the Modernisation Scheme. The Class 40's inherent design fault – its liability to bogie fractures – has caused problems and much expense for BR and has been the downfall of numerous members of the class once withdrawals began.

Only the Southern Region did not see regular appearances of this heavy workhorse – a surprising fact considering the proximity of London-based locomotives on the LMR and ER. By comparison, Severn Tunnel Junction has been a frequent destination for the class with LM-originating freights.

The resurrection by BR of 40122, the original D200, in 1983 was a commendable decision and brought BR much deserved praise. Although D200 was returned to service for commercial reasons, it was a fitting commemoration of the service that this class has rendered and should surely guarantee rightful preservation of this historic locomotive, the first Type 4 built for the Modernisation Scheme.

The twilight years of the class have been marked by the growing appreciation of enthusiasts and several locomotives are earmarked for preservation, although some private railways view with apprehension the prospect of such weight on certain bridges! The following pages portray the life and times of the Class 40 over a quarter of a century and provide a reminder of the variety of routes and services which this class has worked, many of which have already passed into history. During the years, and perhaps unexpectedly for a diesel class, several members have become celebrities, either notoriously or deservedly, and some of these will be found herein.

The stylish nameplate of D215. The naming of certain LMR-allocated Class 40s after ocean liners was, in hindsight, a commendable policy decision for the design and names added considerable panache and quality appreciation to these locomotives: so much so, that 20 years later the survivors of those so named began to acquire painted versions of the originals, albeit in ordinary straight nameplate style. D215 had its nameplates fitted in May 1962 but, together with those of its sisters, had them removed in the 1960s due, it is believed, to difficulties with washing machines. (*Hugh Ballantyne*)
Voigtlander CLR   50mm   f2.8 Skopar
Agfa CT18   1/60, f8

It is with many thanks that the kind assistance of fellow Class 40 devotee and connoisseur, Howard Johnston, is acknowledged, and both Ken Harris of Jane's and I would like to thank the photographers who provide such a feast of memories. We hope the selection of these pictures recalls fond memories and provides a lasting tribute to this long-lived locomotive class.

MURRAY BROWN
Harrogate
December 1983

Vintage memories are recalled in this scene at Bethnal Green on 28 February 1959 depicting the first route to have English Electric Company Type 4 power on its main services – the GE main line to Norwich. In charge of the 1230 Liverpool Street to Norwich is No D205, one of the Stratford-based locomotives renowned for their cleanliness. D205 and its four sisters (D200/2/3/4) were the pride of Stratford for nine years until displaced by Class 47s. This locomotive had the dubious distinction of being one of the first batch to be condemned, on 24 January 1976, and met its end at Crewe Works the following year. (R C Riley)
Agfa Super Silette   f2 Solagon
Kodachrome 8   1/250, f2

Above. D351 pictured at York. It was delivered in July 1961 and allocated to York depot, being part of the then North Eastern Region batch Nos D345–D356. The locomotive survived until withdrawal in April 1981 and was cut up at Swindon in September 1982.

Note the Metro-Cammell DMU in the Harro-gate bay platform and the beautiful Thompson coach with its distinctive oval white windows immediately behind the locomotive. (*Colin Boocock*)
Voigtlander Vito IIa   *Agfa CT18*

Right. Happy memories! Kings Cross in the early 1960s. D279, delivered new to Gateshead depot in June 1960, pounds out of 'The Cross' on 18 March 1961. Over twenty years later this locomotive was still giving loyal service and was based at Longsight, Manchester. (*R C Riley*)
Agfa Super Silette
Kodachrome 8   1/250, f2

Left. How many of you have savoured scenes such as this on a freezing platform before cocooning yourself in a real steam-heated night express? The 2300 Kings Cross–Leeds on 14 September 1981 had in charge No 40069. Remember it with affection for it is no more, having been condemned and broken up within weeks at Doncaster Works, almost before it was cold. (*Howard Johnston*)
Olympus OM1   Ektachrome 200
20 secs, f11

Above. It would be unforgivable not to include a photographic tribute to a train which ran for many years with Class 40 haulage, was one of the longest out and home workings and which required and produced prodigious feats of haulage with some huge tonnages – the York–Inverness Motorail service. The York locomotive worked throughout, returning with the southbound service the following evening. No 40083 conserves its energy for the job ahead in No 3 bay platform at York on 23 September

1981. This was the locomotive which was hauling the 0240 Cliffe–Uddingston cement train which derailed at Cod Beck, Thirsk on 31 July 1967 and into which ploughed the highly successful EE prototype locomotive DP2. Withdrawal for No 40083 came in November 1981, only two months after this picture. (*Barry Plues*)
Pentax SP1000   Agfachrome 100
30 secs, f5.6

The growing interest which inevitably accompanies the impending withdrawal of a class manifested itself in the Class 40s during the 1980s with locomotives being specially cleaned for railtours and Open Days. No 40092 displays such evidence as it plods up to Standedge from Huddersfield on 23 October 1982 with coal from Monkton to Oakley Sidings. (*John S Whiteley*)
Olympus OM1   85mm   Kodachrome 64

No 40176, new to Camden in February 1962, is pictured four months from withdrawal on menial duties at Elland, on the former L & Y main line. The permanent way train was in use for repairs to Elland tunnel on 24 April 1981. In May 1982, 40176, one of the batch fitted with the initial variant of dual brake equipment, was hauled on its last journey to Swindon. (*Gavin Morrison*)

*Pentax SP1000   Kodachrome 25
1/250, f2.8*

Left. Early days at Camden depot when the future Class 40s were the dominant traction units for the WCML. This view was taken on 18 March 1961 with No D268 in the centre of the limelight sporting the 'Ulster Express' headboard. At this time it was a Crewe locomotive, having been delivered there in March 1960. In the period 1981–3, No 40068 was a popular machine for railtours. (*R C Riley*)
Agfa Super Sillette
F2 Solagon
Kodachrome 8   1/60, f2

Left. The second of the LMR's Camden batch, D211, reposes on '1B' after delivery on 30 May 1959. All the Class 40s were accepted on the Eastern Region as this was the sponsoring Region. (Each locomotive class had a sponsoring Region which was in charge of monitoring performance and whose representative chaired the meetings where the class was assessed.) Following crew training, D211 and its sisters were to begin the onslaught of the West Coast Main Line steam fleet. It was named *Mauretania* by Sir J L Brocklebank, Chairman of the Cunard Steamship Company, at Liverpool Riverside on 20 September 1960 and, uniquely for a namer, ended its days on the ER at Healey Mills. Condemned in October 1980, 40011 was cut up at Swindon in the same year. (*Colin Boocock*)
Voigtlander Vito IIa
Agfa CT18

Born January 1961, died February 1981, D316 offers a magnificent sight by which to remember the Class 40s. Queensville curve, Stafford is the setting as D316 wheels through a down parcels on 6 October 1962. *(Michael Mensing)*
Voigtlander Bessa II   Color Heliar f3.5
High Speed Ektachrome   1/500, f5.4

Probably the most famous or notorious Class 40 of the fleet is No 40126 which, as D326, will always be remembered as the Great Train Robbery engine. D326 was heading the 1850 Aberdeen/Glasgow to Euston on 8 August 1963 when the train robbers relieved the GPO of £2½m at Sears Crossing, north of Cheddington. As a result No D326 was impounded by the police! This machine was placed on a 'hit list' of likely locomotives for withdrawal in the autumn of 1983 in view of minor defects which would eventually require major expenditure, but the locomotive soldiered on to the end of 1983, escaping doom by dint of some of its sisters failing with more serious faults and thus being condemned in lieu.

No 40126 is pictured on a cement train working from Earles Sidings on the Hope Valley line on 9 August 1983. The location is Chinley. (*John Day*)
Pentax K1000
Fujichrome R100

Chester has been a favourite location for this venerable class for many years until withdrawals reduced appearances noticibly from 1983. The North Wales coast line through Chester has reverberated to the much loved sound since many readers were in short trousers! No 40111 was in charge of a troop train from Gairloch Head to Bangor on this sunny day, 15 September 1979, and is seen leaving Chester. This locomotive, one of the RSH batch, was new to Crewe as D311 in December 1960. Unusually stored from November 1975 until January 1976, it was reprieved until May 1981 and broken up at Swindon in February 1982. (*Hugh Ballantyne*)

Leica M3   50mm f2 Summicron
Kodachrome 25   1/250, f2.8/4

Above. A far cry from its inaugural BR duties when, as D209, this locomotive was one of Hornsey's (later Finsbury Park's) top link traction units, this veteran, now soldiering on as No 40009, shunts at Penmaenmawr on 31 May 1983 after arrival from St Helens with an engineering trip working.

No 40009 became a celebrity in 1983 when it survived long enough to become the final vacuum-braked Class 40 in service, a negative qualification. Indeed, because of its operational distinction, it appeared on a list of Class 40 locomotives earmarked for early withdrawal but, because of its determination not to fail with a serious defect, continued to defy condemnation orders and enjoyed daily sorties mainly in the Manchester area. It also attracted serious interest from one of the private railways, whose hopeful intention to purchase this locomotive will provide a fitting reward for 25 years service. (*John Chalcraft*)
Mamiya 645   Sekor 80mm
Agfa R100S

Opposite. This picture graphically portrays that one does not need a steam locomotive to make a marvellous celluloid masterpiece! The line is the picturesque Conway Valley line from Llandudno Junction to Blaenau Ffestiniog and the train is the daily pick-up, near Roman Bridge. The one Railfreight wagon conveys ICI explosives from their factory at Penrhyndeudraeth (spelt correctly only when sober!). In charge on this day, 11 August 1983, was No 40004, one of the 25-year-old veterans of the class, and forever remembered as one of the elite Stratford allocation. No 40004 has been LMR-allocated since April 1966. (*Les Nixon*)
Pentax 6 × 7   Takumar 105mm
Ektachrome 200   1/500, f5.6

Left. Heading the up 'Ulster Express' on 25 June 1961 is D302, seven months after being delivered new to Crewe diesel depot. It is pictured leaving Beechwood tunnel between Birmingham and Coventry, having been diverted from the Trent Valley line. D302 was the locomotive loaned to Leeds, Neville Hill depot in January 1961 in preparation for receipt of its own allocation of Class 40s – the famed 'Queen of Scots' batch, Nos D345–48. No 40102 as it duly became was amongst the first 'Whistlers' to be condemned in January 1976. It was finally cut up in Crewe works in January 1977. *(Michael Mensing)*
Hasselblad 1000F
Tessar f2.8
Agfa CT18
1/1000, f2.8

Right. D334 was always a LMR locomotive. It was delivered new to Crewe in March 1961 and spent its working life at various depots on the region until condemnation in May 1981. Despatch to Swindon for an inevitable fate occurred in December of the same year. Pictured in happier times on a renowned Class 40 route, the North Wales coast line, D334 was in charge of the London–Holyhead day mail train when this photograph was taken on 28 August 1964, with the unmistakable skyline of Conway providing the backdrop. *(Derek Cross)*
Linhof Technika
Agfa CT18
1/250, f5.6

Haymarket depot received two allocations of this class, D260–66 (40060–66) and D357–68 (40157–68). Examples of both batches, Nos 40066 and 40160, pose in this portrait taken on 2 September 1979. No 40066, like its sisters, was retrospectively fitted with headcode panels like the 40157–66 allocation, and was one of the three Class 40s never to be transferred during its BR life, which came to an end in April 1981. *(Gavin Morrison)*
Pentax SP1000   Kodachrome 25
1/250, f3.5

This delightful setting is Montrose viaduct, in one of the long-established Class 40 domains. No 40168, delivered in December 1961 to form the last of the initial allocations to Haymarket passes over this impressive structure on 18 April 1981 with an up Aberdeen–Glasgow express. After 20 years at Haymarket, 40168 moved to Longsight in October 1981. (*Gavin Morrison*)

Pentax SP1000   *Kodachrome 25*
1/250, f3.5

19

Left. A NER and later ER locomotive until 1983, when it moved to the LMR, No 40152 heads through the picturesque Princes Street Gardens, Edinburgh on 7 June 1975 with a cement train from Oxwellmains. (*John S Whiteley*)
Pentax SP2   85mm
Kodachrome 25

Right. Around the country are some very well known vantage points for photography and, in the case of Class 40s, audio entertainment! The climb from Inverkeithing to North Queensferry is one of the favourite locations and No 40159 was testing vision and acoustics on 21 April 1981 with an up Aberdeen–Edinburgh express. A Haymarket locomotive for most of its life, it is noteworthy for one unusual episode during its 21-year life in that it was allocated to Immingham, 40B, from November 1972 to May 1973. Swindon Works was its final destination and it departed from this world in September 1983. (*Gavin Morrison*)
Pentax SP1000
Kodachrome 25
1/250, f3.5

A beautiful picture epitomising the early years of the EE Type 4s. No D261 was one of the original Haymarket batch (D260–66) and spent much of its life south of the border working Anglo-Scottish freights and passenger turns. This batch was, as shown in the picture, fitted with discs but these were later removed in favour of a central headcode panel. D261 was finally transferred away from Haymarket in May 1981 and has latterly found comfort at Carlisle depot.

On a superb summer's evening, D261 heads the 7.57 pm Berwick on Tweed–Edinburgh just north of the border. The date was 30 May 1962. (*Michael Mensing*)
Hasselblad 1000F   Tessar f2.8
Ektachrome High Speed   1/1000, f3.5

Spot the difference! Yes, it is the same locomotive, D261, but sporting its new headcode panel. The Haymarket series D260–66 was altered in this fashion commencing in 1965, removal of the gangway doors being necessary to accommodate this modification. This view of D261 was taken on 29 June 1966 at the popular photographic location of Princes Street Gardens, Edinburgh and shows a traffic which regularly provided work for the 64B-allocated Type 4s and which brought them south of the border practically every day – the Aberdeen–London express goods. (*Derek Cross*)
Linhof Technika   Agfa CT18 Professional 1/250, f5.6

23

Left. A view of the Newcastle to Carlisle line, used by the Class 40s for over two decades. Haltwhistle is the location of this picture of No 40140 on 25 February 1979 heading west with the 1100 Tyne Yard–Carlisle Yard, a special freight following ASLEF action. New to Crewe in April 1961, this locomotive was condemned in March 1982 and was sent to Derby Works for scrap. However, a change of decision resulted in 40140 being hauled to Crewe, where it was cut up in August 1983. (*Mrs D A Robinson*)
Pentax 6 × 7   Ektachrome 200
1/500, f5.6

Above. The Haverton Hill (Teesside)–Leith ammonia tank train has for many years been a favourite train for Class 40 photographers, and no wonder if this view taken on 19 September 1979 is typical. This train has regularly been a Class 40 turn and, indeed, has continued to produce these machines even after their elimination from the ER. No 40133 is the star performer in this picture taken at Houndwood. It was new to Crewe in February 1961 as D333 and despite being put on a 'hit list' in the autumn of 1983, continued to evade withdrawal. (*Mrs D A Robinson*)
Pentax 6 × 7   Ektachrome 200
1/500, f6.3

Above. Remember the Heaton–Manchester Red Bank van train in steam days, so often the preserve of a double-header? This train has continued to run through the succeeding years with regular Class 40 haulage. In this view taken at Ferryhill on 10 February 1980, No 40067 bowls along in the winter afternoon sunshine with this time-honoured train, the 1306 (Sun) from Heaton. *(Mrs D A Robinson)*
Pentax 6 × 7   Ektachrome 200
1/1000, f4

Right. Another of the original Haymarket allocation, No 40160 is pictured on a route which has long been familiar territory for the Class 40s, the North-East coast line via Sunderland and Hartlepool. The train is 3B01, the 1721 Sunderland Brian Mills Depot–Peterborough parcels and is seen at Monkwearmouth on 2 July 1979. First allocated to Haymarket in September 1961, No 40160 has been a LMR locomotive since 1973. *(Peter J Robinson)*
Pentax 6 × 7   Ektachrome 200
1/500, f6.3

Left. This countryside has reverberated to Class 40 music since 1958 – the Northumberland section north of Morpeth. D354 thunders northbound with a bulk cement train, probably the Cliffe to Uddingston train which would have been hauled to York by a pair of SR Class 33 locomotives, near Beal on 31 May 1962. This locomotive is but a memory, having been withdrawn in May 1982. When based at York, where it arrived new in July 1961, it was loaned to March in October 1961 in preparation for through workings by the class to and from East Anglia. *(Michael Mensing)*
Hasselblad 1000F
Tessar f2.8   Agfa CT18
1/1000, f4

Right. The up morning 'Talisman' arrives at Berwick-on-Tweed on 1 June 1962 headed by No D256, probably deputising for a Deltic. This locomotive's claim to fame is that following delivery to York depot in January 1960, it was loaned to Haymarket together with Nos D257 and D258, the first Class 40s to go north of the border for crew training. No 40056 as it eventually became survived a trip to Crewe Works in late 1982 and is thus assured to be one of the last survivors. *(Michael Mensing)*
Hasselblad 1000F
Tessar 2.8
Agfacolour CT18
1/1000, f3.5

Above. If there are Edinburgh-bound excursions, probably power will be a Class 40, although in recent years the class has been gradually giving way to Class 45s and Class 47s. No 40052 heads such a train on the Penmanshiel deviation on the morning of 26 May 1980. Allocated new to York in December 1959, this locomotive was one of the last Eastern Region 40s to receive the blue livery in the early 1970s. It was withdrawn in June 1983 and was cut up at Crewe in November of that same year. (*Peter J Robinson*)
Pentax 6 × 7   Ektachrome 200 1/1000, f4.5

Right. Many long distance holiday expresses have been the preserve of the Class 40s for over two decades. The August exodus of Glaswegians is catered for with the running of Glasgow–Scarborough trains and one of the original Haymarket-allocated locomotives, No 40161, powers the 0810 from Glasgow past Pegswood, Northumberland on 23 August 1980. This locomotive's claim to fame, together with sister Nos 40165 and 40066, is that these locomotives were the only 40s never to be transferred. Following withdrawal four months after this picture was taken, No 40161 was broken up at Swindon in June 1981. (*Peter J Robinson*)
Pentax 6 × 7   Ektachrome 200 1/1000, f5.6

The former CLC shed at Northwich plays host to No 40099 on the evening of 4 August 1983. On some members of the class, the water tank to feed the steam-heating boiler has been removed to leave the unsightly void between the bogies which is evident in this view. *(R T Osborne)*
Canon AE/1   100 mm
Kodachrome 64
1/125, f4–5.6

Garston, has been a haunt of the Class 40s for many years. Resting between duties at Garston stabling point on 24 June 1975 were Nos 40105, 40063, 40106 and 40116. *(Barry J Nicolle)*
Pentax SP2   Agfa CT18
1/125, f5.6

When 40136 was painted blue, this left 40106 the sole green Class 40. Because of this, it became a celebrity and much to the delight of the railway world was repainted green at its classified repair in 1978, a surprising event considering the usual rigid adherence to the corporate image. When the state of 40106's bogies and the fact that it was vacuum-braked only brought about its withdrawal in 1983, sufficient interest in this long-lived machine led BR to offer the locomotive for sale by tender, and it is to see out the rest of its working days on the Great Central Railway at Loughborough. This is how No 40106 appeared after its repainting in 1978, a green oasis amid a sea of blue! The location – Chester. The date – 7 October 1978. (*Gavin Morrison*)
Pentax SP1000   Kodachrome 25
1/250, f2.8

This is D216 *Campania*, four and a half miles south-east of Weedon, providing power for a Carlisle train on 12 April 1963. D216 is a star in all respects. It was new to Crewe in June 1959, the first of its type to be shedded there. Only nine days after this picture was taken it was seriously damaged in the Kings Langley crash when it unfortunately hit an electrification crane whilst working the 1220 Holyhead–Euston. This locomotive was also one of the nominated 'Royal' Class 40s and often shared these important duties with No D233 even though there was more modern power available. One such duty included Royal Train service during the Prince of Wales' Investiture at Caernarvon Castle on 1 July 1969. Withdrawn in May 1981, it was broken up at Swindon in November 1983. *(Michael Mensing)*
Voigtlander Bessa II
Colour Heliar f3.5   High Speed Ektachrome
1/500, f5.6

No D308 was destined to be a LMR locomotive all its life. Built at Darlington by RSH in 1960, it began its 20-year reign at Crewe depot. In August 1980, withdrawal took place and No 40108, as it was then, was towed to Swindon for breaking, a task completed in December 1980. This beautiful evening sun portrait of the locomotive when it was less than one year old was taken west of Brinklow, on the Trent Valley line, and vividly conveys the atmosphere of the early years of this class. The train was the 1640 Euston–Stafford 'stopper' and the date was 6 August 1961. (*Michael Mensing*)
Hasselblad 1000F   Tessar f2.8
Agfa CT18   1/500, f3.2

35

Above. The last of the split headcode batch, No 40144, climbs the bank up to Golborne Junction on the WCML with a southbound fitted freight on 2 May 1980. Edge Hill, Liverpool was D344's first home and this locomotive spent its life at LMR depots. Condemned in May 1981, it departed from this world at Swindon Works in September 1983. *(R T Osborne)*
Canon AE/1   Kodachrome 64

Left. This locomotive spent 20 years based on NER territory before becoming a LMR responsibility in mid-1982. New to Gateshead in July 1962, No 40197 achieved a curious claim to fame when its boiler, isolated for many years, was surprisingly reinstated: surprisingly, because it was a Clayton boiler, the only operational one of its type left on the class, and when the locomotive was transferred to the LMR this soon became an operating inconvenience in view of its singularity. The locomotive came to the end of its life at the conclusion of 1983. It is pictured enjoying its last few months at Acton Grange, Moore on 21 July 1983 in charge of Ravenscraig–Dee Marsh steel coil train. *(R T Osborne)*
Canon AE/1   Kodachrome 64

This picture of No 40191 epitomises the type of duty on which the surviving dual-braked Class 40s have spent much of their twilight years – block company trains. The 1340 SO Corkickle–Northwich empties hurries past Bamfurlong on the WCML. The date was 18 April 1981. No 40191 – a nondescript Class 40? Not quite! Would you believe that a Class 40 was actually allocated on the WR? No 40191 was officially based at Hereford from June 1977 to November of that year. (R T Osborne)
Canon AE/1   Kodachrome 64

Above. A picturesque and little photographed route which has long been a stamping ground for the 'Whistlers' is the Cumbrian Coast line. This line has for many years provided an alternative to the West Coast Main Line, both for diversionary purposes and for easing congestion on the WCML, although loading gauge restrictions rather limit its use. No 40074, one of the original Gateshead machines (May 1960), is seen in charge of the 1730 Workington–Dover Speedlink at Netherton on 16 August 1983. At this time it was still an ER locomotive but was included amongst the last five on the ER transferred to the LMR in October 1983. (*Mrs D A Robinson*)
*Pentax 6 × 7   Ektachrome 200
1/500, f6.3*

Right. Banked by two Class 20s, No 40165 restarts the Winsford to Millerhill block salt train out of Beattock loop on 1 August 1979. This train had been diverted from the ECML due to the Penmanshiel tunnel blockage. This locomotive remained allocated to Haymarket throughout its life and was condemned in June 1981. It spent the next two years on the Eastern Region as a 'Christmas Tree' (yielding spares) at York and Immingham depots before meeting its inevitable end at Doncaster Works in June 1983. (*Peter J Robinson*)
*Pentax 6 × 7   Ektachrome 200
1/250, f8*

Left. How many can recognise this 1964 view of Elvanfoot? The coming of the wires has drastically changed the scene since D309 was captured on film powering a Glasgow to Liverpool express on 26 March 1964. One of the RSH-built Class 40s, D309 was a Crewe-allocated locomotive when delivered in November 1960 and was withdrawn in December 1980. (*Derek Cross*)

Linhof Technika   Agfa CT18   1/250, f5.6

Above. Another classic Class 40 route – without the experience of which afficionados of this class have deprived themselves of pure pleasure – is the Stranraer road. This scene depicts a car special leaving the outskirts of Ayr at Dalrymple Junction on 2 July 1966 in the capable hands of No D369. A popular locomotive with enthusiasts, D369 was one of the final trio allocated to Crewe in December 1961. Last overhauled at Crewe Works in December 1979, it was eventually withdrawn in December 1983 after persistent works visits through failures. (*Derek Cross*)

Linhof Technika   Agfa CT18   1/250, f5.6

Left. As this book was compiled in 1983, enthusiasts searching for the last of the 'Whistlers' were heading for the Manchester area to savour the vanishing delights of the English Electric 16SVT power unit, not forgetting no fewer than four turbochargers to go with it!

Guide Bridge is as good as any location to wallow in 'Whistlers' and this picture of No 40128 on eastbound HBA hoppers taken on 3 June 1981 will no doubt bring back many memories to many readers. Condemned in September 1982, No 40128 had no dignity in death for it was garishly painted to partake in an exhibition at Stockport. Doncaster Works laid this Class 40 to rest in August 1983. (*Howard Johnston*)

Olympus OM1   Ektachrome 64   1/250, f8

Below. 40118. How it survived is one of life's great mysteries for it spent many months out of service in Crewe Works, only to re-enter days after coming out for a further spell under repair. 40118's penchant for Crewe Works thus made the locomotive a very rare machine for the haulage fans. When this picture was taken, it had become the last RSH Darlington-built locomotive in traffic. It stands at Blackpool on 8 July 1981 with a Preston train. (*Howard Johnston*)

Praktica LB2   Ektachrome 64   1/125, f8

A classic location but one of which you never tire! Helwith Bridge, scene of countless heroic locomotive battles, is overlooked by Penyghent as No 40094 pounds over the River Ribble with a down freight on 26 August 1981. This Class 40 was new to Crewe in September 1960 and was given maintenance hospitality on Scottish, Eastern and Midland depots during its BR service, which ended with withdrawal in April 1982. (*Gavin Morrison*)
Pentax SP1000   *Kodachrome 25*
1/250, f2.8

Left. Epitaph for the Class 40s could easily be the fond memories of the performances of the 'Whistlers' on the Settle & Carlisle. This poignant view of two life-expired 40s (one had indeed failed) on the life-expired Ribblehead viaduct reminds us all that there are only two certainties in life – death and taxation! Performers on this Carlisle–Bescot freight on 21 August 1980 were Nos 40163 and 40179. (*John S Whiteley*)
Pentax SP2   85mm   Kodachrome 25

Above. Now, be honest. Wouldn't you do the same, having seen such a marvellous sight on Ribblehead? A quick 'bomb' down to Hellifield with five minutes to spare produces another beautiful picture of Nos 40163 and 40179 turning off the MR main line and heading for Blackburn. (*John S Whiteley*)
Pentax SP2   85mm   Kodachrome 25

Left. Meanwhile on the southbound duty of 'The Royal Scot' on the same day came a surprise – NER-allocated D253, commandeered for the LMR's prestige train. Did Gateshead know?! The location is Shap Quarry Sidings. D253 was a York locomotive when new in January 1960 and was sent to Leith early in its life to prepare crews for the allocation of Class 40s to Haymarket. Condemned in August 1976, 40053 was cut up at Crewe in April 1977. (*Rodney A Lissenden*) *Rolliecord Vb   Agfa CT18*

Below left. The classic setting for a classic train – 'The Royal Scot'. No D325, the first of the split headcode variety does battle with Shap on 20 July 1963. New to Crewe in December 1960, D325, later to become 40125, was always LMR-allocated. This locomotive met its end at Swindon in November 1983. (*Rodney A Lissenden*) *Rolliecord Vb   Agfa CT18*

Opposite. D241 was one of the first Class 40s to be withdrawn, being condemned in July 1976 and cut up at Crewe in December 1978. It was allocated new to Gateshead in October 1959 and gave service to three Regions – NER, LMR and ScR. This picture shows D241 with full yellow warning panel on the up 'Thames–Clyde Express' at Kirkconnel on 12 April 1971. (*Derek Cross*) *Linhof Technika Agfa CT18 Professional 1/250, f5.6*

Left. Following the success of the four Deltic locomotives nominated to work enthusiasts' specials, the ER CM&EE at York chose two Class 40s to be similarly treated, Nos 40057 and 40084. Both locomotives at the time (1982) were allocated to Gateshead depot, which was duly awarded the task of sprucing them up. Shortly after this unexpected bonus for photographers had been completed, No 40057 was given a day out on the Edinburgh–Carlisle via Newcastle and return. It is pictured at Greenhead on the Carlisle–Newcastle line on 10 May 1982. No 40057 was new in February 1960 (at York depot) and was one of the last five ER Class 40s based at Healey Mills before being sent to the LMR in October 1983. (*Mrs D A Robinson*)
Pentax 6 × 7
Ektachrome 200
1/1000, f4

Right. The two 'Gateshead Specials' on their first railtour. The date was 8 May 1982 and the immaculate pair is seen passing Dorn, near Moreton-in-Marsh, with 'The Cotswold Venturer'. This special was run by Severn Valley Railtours and full credit must be given to them for not ruining the front locomotive with a silly headboard! Sadly, No 40084 suffered bogie troubles in May 1983 and we must now remember it with pictures such as this one. (*Peter J Skelton*)
Hasselblad 500CM
Ektachrome 64   1/500, f4

Left. 1905 to Mossend. By the summer of 1983, once frequent Class 40 workings into the Western Region from Crewe had almost vanished, having been replaced by Class 47 haulage.

A telephone call to Severn Tunnel Junction depot on 2 September 1983 confirmed a Class 40 had worked downside for the evening Mossend and a wait at Caerleon was rewarded with this beautifully lit view of No 40167, the last Class 40 to receive a Classified Repair (Intermediate) at Crewe Works as late as February 1981, on the 1905 to Mossend. (*Derek Short*)
Mamiya 645   150mm Mamiya-Sekor
1/125, f4   Agfa R100S

Below. It is a balmy summer's evening, with the crickets chirping in the grass. A pigeon coos occasionally, mixing with the drone of an aircraft from Linton in the distance, and then is heard the rumble of an unmistakable sound. This time-honoured scene is probably the one by which the editor will remember the Class 40s when they are no more, having spent countless hours alongside this magnificent stretch of railway, the 44 miles of racing track north of York. On 20 July 1982, No 40198 was caught ambling along the slow line at Shipton, approaching Skelton on the outskirts of York. No 40198 was sent brand new to Gateshead depot and spent twenty years based at former NER depots before accepting hospitality at Longsight in October 1982. Condemned in 1983, No 40198 had a strange duty before proceeding to Doncaster Works: it was one of two Class 40s which were used as weights for bridge testing at Spalding. (*Barry Plues*)
Pentax SP1000   SMC Takumar 135mm
Kodachrome 64   1/250, f3.5

York ranks with Crewe as top Class 40 territory and even after October 1983 when the last five ER 40s left for the LMR, examples could still be seen at this mecca. This appropriate sunset portrait shows Nos 40061 and 40052 leaving York Yard with a southbound oil tank train from Tees-side on 21 July 1982. (*Barry Plues*)

Kodachrome 64   1/250, f4

Pentax SP1000   SMC Takumar 135mm

Left. D330 and D296 doublehead the 1210 Birmingham New Street–Bangor on Sunday 11 April 1965. The train is passing the site of Ocker Hill station on the Tipton to Walsall section, diverted from the Stour Valley line while electrification work proceeded. D330 spent its life allocated on the LMR, being withdrawn in March 1982 and cut up in May 1983. *(Michael Mensing)*
Nikkorex F   Agfacolour CT18
1/1000, f2.5

Above. A rare view from the past is this study of No D318 approaching Wednesbury tunnel on the GWR Birmingham–Wolverhampton line on a Sunday evening, 24 April 1966. The train is the 1725 Birmingham Snow Hill (altered from New Street)–Liverpool and Manchester, diverted on account of electrification works. D318, one of the Robert Stephenson Hawthorn batch built at Darlington (Nos D305–24), was chosen to play the leading part in the film 'Robbery', based on the Great Train Robbery, where it emulated D326, a curious choice for the part as D326 has split indicators! Nearly two decades after this photograph, No 40118, as it had become, achieved further notoriety – see page 42. *(Michael Mensing)*
Nikkorex F   Agfacolour CT18
1/500, f3

Left. Air-braked services to Parkeston have brought Class 40s to East Anglia in their later years, a reminder of the pioneering GE main line days of these locomotives. With a train formation that would look more at home in northern France than Essex, No 40158 nears journey's end at Mistley on 14 August 1980 with the 2135 Mossend–Parkeston ABS. (*R T Osborne*)
Canon AE/1   Kodachrome 64

Above. A look at the life and times of the Class 40s would not be complete without a portrait taken on what was, for many years, a favourite stomping ground for the 'Whistlers', the holiday route of the 'Joint' line from Doncaster through Lincoln and Sleaford to March. Pictured at Sleaford on 11 September 1982 is No 40030 in charge of the 0818 (SO) Manchester–Skegness. Although LMR-based Class 40s have long worked into Whitemoor Yard, March, the summer Saturday holiday trains from Manchester have provided Class 40 fans with more opportunities for haulage in recent years. (*John Chalcraft*)
Mamiya 645   80mm   Agfa R100S

Veteran No 40001 sets back its train from Mountsorrel at West Yard, Peterborough on 28 July 1983. When, as no D201, this locomotive first hauled 'The Flying Scotsman' through Peterborough in June 1958, A2s, K3s and 9Fs would have been prominent in nearby New England depot. By the date of this picture 40001 was a celebrity of a different kind: with sister D200 having spent more than a year out of action at Carlisle before restoration, 40001 was the longest continuously serving member of the class. (*John Rudd*)

Nikon EM   50 mm   Kodachrome 64 f5.6, auto

The last of the RSH-built hatch, No 40124, heads north from Peterborough on 20 June 1983 with train 6S93, the Parkeston Quay–Paisley Speedlink service. Leading the consist are five Procar 80s conveying imported cars, followed by a long string of VGA vans from Wisbech. *(John Rudd)*
Nikon EM   50 mm   Kodachrome 64 f4, auto

57

Above. Gargrave is the setting for this 1970 view of a Healey Mills–Carlisle freight preparing shortly to do battle with the 'Long Drag'. The unidentified Class 40 was photographed on 7 March of that year and still sports its grimy green livery. (*John S Whiteley*)
Minolta SR1   55mm   Kodachrome 2

Right. Hellifield is now part of the past, when Britain really did have a railway system. Its grandiose station, nowadays decaying, is a reminder of the times when the Midland Main Line saw vast amounts of traffic, including diversions from the WCML. It is ironic that despite the run-down of the Settle & Carlisle line, this route is still regularly used for diver-

sionary purposes. D339 was on such duty on 4 August 1968 when it headed the 1M23 Edinburgh–Birmingham past this bleak outpost of Midland Railway indulgence. This locomotive hauled its last train in February 1982. (*Derek Cross*)
Linhof Technika   Agfa CT18   1/250, f5.6

Left. No 40095 is the subject of this study. As D295, this locomotive was first shedded at Crewe in September 1960. It is seen on duty on the Settle & Carlisle, standing at Garsdale on 14 April 1981 with one of the vacuum-braked freights for which the line was used during the rapid changeover to air-braked trains. As for No 40095, only five months after performing this working, it suffered fire damage and was condemned, meeting its end at Swindon Works in October 1983. (*Les Nixon*)
Pentax 6 × 7
Takumar 105mm
Agfa CT18
1/125, f6.3

Right. The Settle & Carlisle is one of those lines synonymous with the magnificent audio entertainment of this class and, indeed, a Class 40 had the dubious distinction of hauling the final booked freight working in 1983. Memories of happier times for this line and class are captured in this view of No 40084 on freight duty on 15 April 1981. The location is Moorcock tunnel. As outlined on page 49 this locomotive was later to become a railtour celebrity until its demise in 1983. (*Les Nixon*)
Pentax 6 × 7
Takumar 150mm
Ektachrome 200
1/500, f5.6

Below. Without a doubt, a collector's gem of a picture. This is the now legendary D200, alias 40122, parked outside Toton depot on 23 July 1983. Having posed the previous day as D200 without yellow warning panels, the depot staff were only too pleased to apply the earlier style small panels (not quite correctly, but never mind) for literally a few hours, after which the locomotive received its obligatory full yellow ends. Indeed, the staff could not be praised sufficiently. When asked if the locomotive was to receive white tyres, the reply was, 'Do you want us to paint them?' Take a bow, Toton! (*Howard Johnston*)
Pentax ME Super
Ektachrome 200
1/250, f5.6

Above. A rare view of the prototype Class 40 outside Crewe Works on 10 May 1970, just after it had received blue livery. This was the era when the 'D' was dropped, prior to introduction of the computer numbering system. Of interest are the BR emblems. It was the practice at Crewe to place two on each side, whilst Derby Works, which overhauled Class 40s for a short period, only placed one. No 200 later took the number 40122, which of course would have been allocated to D322 had it not been involved in the serious collision at Moore on 14 May 1966. (*Hugh Ballantyne*)
Voigtlander CLR
50mm Skopar 2.8
Agfa CT18